BUILDING A CHURCH

A Church Layman's Guide for Navigating the Construction Process

TERRY HARPOOL

ISBN 978-1-64079-749-9 (Paperback)
ISBN 978-1-64079-750-5 (Digital)

Copyright © 2017 by Terry Harpool
All rights reserved. No part of this publication may be reproduced, distributed, or transmitted in any form or by any means, including photocopying, recording, or other electronic or mechanical methods without the prior written permission of the publisher. For permission requests, solicit the publisher via the address below.

Christian Faith Publishing, Inc.
296 Chestnut Street
Meadville, PA 16335
www.christianfaithpublishing.com

Printed in the United States of America

Respectfully dedicated to
John Macon
In deep appreciation for his mentorship

Contents

Foreword 7
1. Prayer Is the Beginning..9
2. Select Your Project Manager and Building Committee 13
3. Determine Your Requirements and Budget 17
4. Selecting Your Architect and Critical Preplanning 21
5. Selecting Your General Contractor 25
6. Church-Managed Subcontractors 35
7. Starting the Construction 39
8. The Dreaded Change Order...47
9. Time, Quality, Money..49
10. Racing to Completion and the Certificate of Occupancy 51
11. Post Construction Maintenance and the Warranty 57
12. Celebrate Your Success!...61

Foreword

Church construction can be one of the most rewarding experiences a Christian can have and one of the most satisfying. It can also truly be a means of worship and fulfillment in helping expand the kingdom of God here on earth. However, it can also be a test of your patience, perseverance, and commitment to the task; prayer is essential throughout the process. It is one of the most glorious feelings when the job is complete and you can stand back and admire a job well done!

In this book I attempt to inform church layman, who may be facing a church construction project, of the many aspects that must be considered when implementing the project. It certainly can be a daunting task especially for a "first timer." And even for the seasoned construction veteran, it can still be a challenge. I hope this book will provide some insight to the many aspects of the construction process and help the project manager, building committee, and church leadership navigate this process in making sound and informed decisions.

The information set forth in this book is based on my own personal experiences as a church project manager for construction. While every new project tends to have a personality of its own, I have narrowed down the most common issues that typically need to be considered in any project. And, these issues should be viewed as the baseline in planning your project.

I wish you great success in your church construction project and pray you too can experience the spiritual blessing of a job "well done."

God Bless,
Terry Harpool

1

Prayer Is the Beginning

At some point in the church, a spark will be set that there is a need for some type of construction in the church. It may be a simple addition to an existing building, it may be a renovation of an existing building, or it may be the construction of an entirely new building. Whatever the case may be, it is critically essential that the first thing the church does is to pray about the Lord's will in the matter. Rushing ahead of God, without earnest and sincere prayer asking for His will and guidance, can result in delays, cost overruns, and confrontation within the church. So by all means, come together as a church and seek God's will long before attempting to start any construction project. I'm certain you will discover His will for construction when you earnestly seek it as a congregation.

There are many ways to start this process. I feel any proposed construction should first be prayed over by a small group within the church, typically the senior staff and elders of the church. Then, the idea for new construction can be expanded to larger groups such as building committees, trustees of the church, or administrative boards. And, as the will of God becomes more defined in time, the church as a whole can be asked to pray for God's will in the proposed construction. Once the entire church is involved in seeking the will of God, there are a variety of ways to get the word out about the new project and inform the congregation.

One approach, which worked very well for my church construction projects, was the "special night event" when the church congregation met to be briefed on the construction proposal. In this case, light snacks were served in a very casual event where the church leadership outlined the proposed construction in an open forum. This gave members the opportunity to ask questions and suggest ideas. This also allowed a dialogue between the church leadership and members of the congregation and allowed everyone to participate in the plan. This is the time when more earnest prayer begins, from the entire congregation, seeking God's will and direction in the proposed church construction.

Typically this kind of approach works very well for single campus churches. However, if the church is a multi-campus congregation, having separate "special night events" at all the campuses is the best approach. And depending on the congregational size of each of the church campuses, the church may elect at first to have special night events by invitation. This allows the church to focus on volunteer leaders within the church and other church staff. And since funding is an essential part of any church construction project, the special night events could also be tailored to personally inform more those who may be able to provide larger financial donations to the construction budget. In any case, the success of the proposed church construction is directly related to how well informed the church congregation is about the project. And with all this information about the project, the congregations knows where to focus their prayer efforts. The congregation must feel like they have a vested interest and personal commitment in the project.

As the church continues to discuss the proposed project and earnestly prays for God's guidance, the church leadership can use a variety of methods to "get the word out" to the congregation. Depending on the capabilities of the church, there can be mailings or posted videos on a church website. At various church services, videos could be shown that portray the need for the new project and how it will benefit the church in expanding the kingdom. One thing that I found helpful was to teach a Sunday school class on the book of Nehemiah. Nehemiah, as you recall, returned from the Babylonian captivity to rebuild the wall around Jerusalem and he faced many obstacles and controversies in that construction project. It helps put in perspective the issues that can occur, and do occur, in any construction effort. The study of Nehemiah also prepares the way for what is involved in construction and how very important it is that the church seeks God's will for the project.

Be prepared, as the church prayerfully seeks God's will, that there may be three possible answers: yes, no, and not now. The "not now" answer is often the hardest one for the congregation and church staff to face. I have observed that even though the answer is "not now," the church leadership often rushes ahead of God into construction. This can be a disaster rooting from poor preplanning and a poorly defined construction timeline resulting in endless issues of poor construction quality during and after the construction phase. Just don't rush ahead of God and remember His timing is not necessarily our timing!

And finally, don't forget to pray as earnestly as a congregation giving thanks to God once the project is complete. Often, the congregation is reveling in the glory of the finished project, and rightfully so, but fail to stop and think about how they got there—by the will and good blessings of God! I would suggest a special service be held to specifically thank God for the blessing of a new facility and ask that He bless the facility for its use in winning souls to Christ. One of the best ways to have this thanksgiving service is by having a grand opening for the new building. Make it a celebration, open the doors to church leaders on and off campus, invite city dignitaries, and advertise to the community your newly completed construction. Specifically offer an open house to the community to show off the facility. It is my experience that many people are most likely to attend a new church facility. So just as the process began with prayer, and continued throughout the project, it should also end with a prayer of thanksgiving.

2

Select Your Project Manager and Building Committee

You have successfully sought God's will in your construction project and now it is time to determine who in the church will manage the project. This will be one of the most critical decisions the church will make, and again, it demands earnest prayer in selecting those chosen to manage the project. In my experience, the best approach is to have a church project manager who oversees the entire project and who is supported by a building committee. I highly recommend whoever is selected for these positions should have some reasonable amount of experience in church construction or program management. It is to the best benefit of the church to have knowledgeable people working and advising on the project.

The project manager (PM) ideally would be someone in the church that has the time and inclination to commit to a long-term project without diversion. In my case, I was a non-paid church volunteer and had the available time and energy to commit to a construction project. Obviously this would be of benefit to the church since a non-paid volunteer would negate a PM salary or fee. Typically contracting a PM position of this type could cost upwards of thirty thousand dollars for a six- to eight-month project. If you don't have such a person in your church, you should consider hiring someone to act as your PM since this person is essential to the smooth operation of your project. In my view, the larger the project the more critical it is the church select someone to fill the position of the PM.

The project manager would be responsible for "riding herd" on all aspects of the construction project. These would include preplanning, architect and general contractor selection, design reviews, daily construction oversight, managing change orders for the project (I will discuss this in a later chapter), maintaining the schedule for construction, authorizing invoice payment, and securing the Certificate of Occupancy from the city or county at the end of the project. The PM would also be responsible for tracking the proposed budget to ensure the church is not overspending in any area. The PM should also provide regular construction status updates to the church administrative boards or staff. In these updates, the PM must be prepared to share the good news as well as the bad for the project. Many good things will happen during construction and those are easy to report, but at times, the project will fall behind schedule or have major issues that will cost the project extra money. I feel it is best to state the true status of the project and try not to sugarcoat any aspect that potentially could cost time or money.

There is also one other very critical aspect of the PM's involvement, which is essential to the smooth operation of the project. I have found in my projects I needed to be on-site every day of construction to see firsthand what was being accomplished (or not being accomplished). The PM is essentially the "eyes and ears" of the church on-site and is available to make on site decisions for the church as needed. Being available to make on-site decisions for the general contractor pays dividends in time by not delaying critical actions that are essential in keeping the project on the timeline. Also, the PM is the extra set of eyes to continually check the design plans against what is being built to assure the general contractor is actually building to design specifications. There have been numerable times in past projects where I caught critical construction errors, and corrected them, long before the discrepancies would have cost the project extra time or money. Again, I cannot over emphasize the presence of the PM on-site every day of the project.

Also, the church PM should be the primary focus of all communication with the project architect and the general contractor. The PM should be empowered to make many construction decisions, which are needed on-site, but also be willing to recognize some decisions need the input of the building committee or church staff. If well-meaning church staff or building committee members communicate directly with the architect or general contractor, without the knowledge of the PM, at the very least, this can result in project delay or even the wrong decision being made. An example of this occurred in one of my projects where a decision needed to be made about a small building design change. A member of the church staff provided one input to the architect, a building committee member provided another input, and the PM provided another input! Needless to say, the architect had no idea what to do and probably wondered who was really managing the project for the church. It does give the impression to professionals in the construction business that the church, as in this example, has no clear lines of communication or authority. Iron this issue out as a church before the project starts so everyone involves the PM in project decisions.

Next, let's look at who should be asked to be members of your building committee. I have found that the PM should be the chairman of this committee. The PM should be the most familiar with the construction design and all aspects of project budget. Given the type of building being constructed, the compliment members of the building committee should reflect the function the building provides for the church. For example, if the church is adding a designated children's area to the church, the committee should include members that have a direct knowledge of children's ministry and children's needs. Their knowledge would be invaluable in design planning of the building. If the church is building a brand new 14,000-square-foot church with a sanctuary, classrooms, and children's ministry areas, then the compliment of the building committee should reflect expertise in all areas of church ministry (i.e., campus pastor, children's minister, building custodian, finance, administrative support, AV/technology, etc.)

In addition to the building committee members listed above, I found church members on the committee who might be general contractors or subcontractors would prove to be invaluable assets. These individuals could provide experienced guidance and advice to the building committee and the PM. People with contractor experience of any kind can provide very helpful reviews of design drawings and often guide the PM through the maze of city or county planning requirements. Also, church members who might hold positions in the local utility companies can be very helpful in cutting through red tape of installing water and power lines for the project. It is important to try and staff the building committee with members that bring specific expertise to the table so they can provide creditable advice to the PM and to the church staff.

Regular meetings and updates to the building committee are imperative to make sure everyone on the committee is informed and aware of the progress. In the age of technology, it is very easy to share pictures and files of the project from start to finish. I tended to keep my committee informed through the email process and met as a group when we had specific issues to resolve. On some issues, which required a vote of the building committee, I would send them a mass email, explain the issue, allow each of them to respond, voice an opinion or make changes, and then ask that they vote yes or no via email to a proposal. This worked very effectively for such things as getting approval to change an exterior paint color. However, for the bigger issues, it was always best to meet as a group to form a consensus.

So, the successful start to any building project is in identifying a capable and qualified PM and selecting building committee members with creditable expertise. This should provide the church with a capable team to oversee the church construction project. And, this team will help keep the project in line with church needs while being cognizant of budget requirements and the project timeline.

3

Determine Your Requirements and Budget

Now that the church has established its need to expand by construction, the church senior staff, project manager, and building committee work as a team to establish the requirements for the project (the function, the size, and the cost). It is so very important these church leaders nail down the exact requirements since this will drive the budget and the construction timeline. As I mentioned earlier, identifying the specific purpose for the expansion is extremely important to make sure the right church experts are brought to the table to help establish the construction requirements.

For example, let's say your church determines it needs to add a wing to the church building to accommodate a growing children's ministry. And, the experts in the church staff and on the building committee determine that the new construction should contain eight classrooms; two rooms for infant care and crawlers, two rooms for toddlers, two rooms for three- to four-year olds, and two rooms for four- to five-year olds. Your children's ministry experts also determines that in the two infant/crawler rooms, each room should have a sink. And, between the two rooms for the toddlers, there should be a shared bathroom with a sink and small child-size toilet. These represent some of the basic requirements the team needs to consider for the new construction.

Additionally, there will be the other kinds of details such as flooring types, room storage options, window size, janitor closets, heating/ventilation/AC (HVAC) types, lighting, door types, etc., all of which must be considered in determining requirements for the construction. In my children's ministry example, inputs from the seasoned veterans in church child care are critical to the process. The requirements list should be discussed over several meetings to make sure the new construction contains all that is needed for the particular function of the building. It is much less expensive to get it right the first time in construction than to go back and modify a completed project after the fact.

Once you have your baseline requirements for your project in place, you can start working an estimate of the cost and considering a budget for the new construction. This is the time having people on the building committee with construction experience can be a real asset to the requirements/budget process. It is possible to estimate the cost per square foot of a building to give you a basic cost for construction of the structure itself. Generally, the church would consider constructing a building with a concrete slab base, wooden studs (metal studs if your budget will allow it), and plywood exterior walls covered in brick. Of course, other options could include exterior wood, metal, or vinyl siding. These are all options, which need to be discussed in the building committee, since they will directly impact how much money the church requires in the construction budget.

I will cover this in later chapters, but the architect or potential general contractor has software tools that will also help to determine the cost of the new construction. In past projects I have managed, I could ask former general contractors to provide a basic cost estimate for constructing a building of specified size and type. Typically, a former contractor is happy to provide this service to the church if they know they may be considered as a potential general contractor to bid the new project. The point of determining cost in the requirements phase is to establish if the church is considering a budget that is too large or even too small to meet the needs of the church.

As the church refines the requirements for the new construction, it isn't too early to start thinking about the other costs of furnishing the new building. Using the example of the new children's wing, the church will need furniture (change tables, rockers, rocker swings, cribs, baby toys, area rugs, movable storage cabinets, trash cans, small tables and chairs, TV and DVD capability, etc.) Furniture costs can be rather high depending on the type of furnishings the church wants in a children's ministry room. Again, the children's ministry experts can be very helpful in determining these costs and adding them to the proposed budget. It is very important to rely on the expertise within the church for the specific ministry the new construction will support!

The requirements and budget should be a bit more defined at this point, but let's also look as associated budgeted areas. As an example, the church may want to include special artwork on the walls of the new children's wing to establish a theme. In all of my projects, the church contracted directly with a mural company to produce a theme for the hallways and classrooms. This would be a cost the church would want to include in the budget estimate. Also, many churches like to include video monitoring in the classrooms and hallways of their children's building to assure security and safety of the children. Again, this would be a cost to add to church's growing budget for new construction.

One very critical budget consideration is the "contingency fund." You never know what issues the church might run into during construction and the additional costs the church might incur. These may include unexpected termite and water damage in a renovation, extra fill dirt to level the ground for construction, repair of the construction site after record-heavy rain falls, or retrofitting a building with fire protection sprinklers due to a city code change. Therefore, the church needs to have a contingency fund, as part of your overall budget, to deal with hidden flaws or unexpected construction costs. I always felt most comfortable if the contingency fund was something near 10 percent of the overall budget (so for a 1.2-million-dollar construction project that would be $120,000). Admittedly, the contingency fund threshold is rather subjective at best. There will be those that feel a much smaller contingency amount would suffice. But my advice is the church should not short itself on the contingency fund amount. Not having the contingency funds budgeted and then needing them can be disastrous for the project. During the contingency budget discussions for new church construction, it would be a good idea to include the church financial managers in this discussion. And ideally include a member of the finance committee as a member of the church building committee.

At this point, the project requirements and budget should be fairly well determined and these need to be presented to the church as a whole. The process for doing this can vary from church to church, but most likely, the requirements and preliminary budget costs will be presented to a church board and then to the entire congregation. Obviously, it is important to have very good estimate to take to the church for their consideration and approval. At these type meetings, the church staff, project manager, building committee, and finance committee members should be available to address questions from the church or church board. These type presentations could be a one-time presentation to the church for a smaller campus, or could be presented numerous times for a multi-campus church. The important point here is to present the most accurate view of the project as possible to the church, so they feel comfortable with the project requirements and budget.

4

Selecting Your Architect and Critical Preplanning

Once the basic requirements list is on hand and the church has a feel for the estimated cost of the construction project, the time is at hand to select a capable architect for the project. There are various ways to select the architect. However, one of the most straightforward ways is for the church to select the same architect, which has provided architectural services for the church on past projects. The advantages of this are the architect's familiarity with the church's architectural preferences and building requirements. But, in the case of a first time construction project, the church can interview several architectural firms to design the new church building.

Since architects provide "professional services," they are not expected to bid against one another for a church architectural contract. This is more of an interview process by the church of the architect's capabilities and an evaluation of the architect's proposed preliminary design. The church should research two or three architectural firms, meet with them individually, discuss the church's requirements for the building, and then ask the architectural firm to present their design ideas to the building committee for the project. The church should request a preliminary design and ask for some basic cost estimate and construction timeline from the architect. These estimates will be helpful in further refining the budget figures and the timeline information will be helpful when selecting a general contractor.

Again, it is very important to thoroughly research any architectural firm to assure they can produce a design beneficial to the church. One of the most basic questions to ask is, "Has the architectural firm designed and built church buildings in the past?" Obviously, it is beneficial to the church if the architect has experience in church construction. Also, ask to see examples of their work in church buildings. For example, it could be the architect only produces ultramodern designs and these may not suit the character of the church. Finally, the church should obtain an estimated architectural fee from the architect for his work in designing and managing the architectural production of the building. The architectural fee estimate is in addition to the cost estimate the architect could provide for construction of the building. This would further help dial in the church's budget estimates for the project. The estimated architectural fee needs to become a firm figure before the architect is selected to design the building and that fee should be clearly stated on any potential architectural contract.

The project manager and members of the church staff need to review the architectural contract, prior to signing, to completely understand the services provided by the architect and the fee for these services. At the very least, the contracted services should include schematic design, design development, construction documents, bidding/negotiating, and construction administration. If the church staff, project manager, or building committee has any questions or concerns about the architectural contract, then meet with the architect to clarify any of the contract services and fees.

After selecting the qualified architect, the preplanning and design phase begins in earnest. This is the time the initial design drawings from the architect will need to be reviewed by the building committee and critical experts in the church staff. This process will be a review of the design with "reds" annotated on the drawings for additions, changes, or deletions. For example, the children's minister may review the design and determine water fountains need to be added in the children's building. Those design changes would then be annotated on the drawings to be incorporated in subsequent preliminary designs. Then these future revised designs would again be reviewed to make sure all the details are incorporated in the design that are critical to the function of the new building. I cannot over emphasize how very important it is to get the details correct in the preliminary design reviews. This will save considerable headaches later in construction by not leaving out some very critical design detail that is essential to the operation of the building. Therefore, a thorough review by church experts will be helpful in making sure those critical details are included in the design. Typically, there will be several reviews of the preliminary design drawings (usually a preliminary review, a 50 percent complete review, and then a 90 percent complete review). And, depending on the size of the project, this review process can take thirty days or longer for all the experts in the church to review and include their changes.

One very important aspect of the design review is to take your time and not rush the review! Again, a steady and committed review of each of the updated drawings will save time and money later during construction. Leaving out a detail (such as forgetting to include water fountains in the children's building) will result in the dreaded change order during construction and this will lead to an additional cost in time and money to the church. Remember, the general contractor will build according to the final approved and signed architectural drawings. If a detail is left out, the church will pay extra during construction to get the detail added back into the design.

Let me add one other word of caution about developing the design drawings for the project. It is so imperative that anyone who is a leader of the church, who might have a say in developing these drawings, be a part of the early design review. They should make their inputs as part of the review team early in the process. What should not happen is for some leader of the church to suddenly insist a major change or addition be added late in the construction of the building. This can cause terrific headaches for the project manager, contractor, and architect by squeezing in a major design change at the last moment. If the change to the design is that critical, it should be discussed very early in the design process and not added "as a matter of fact" late in the construction timeline. Design review and development is a team effort and it should never be circumvented by the veto power of any one individual. Again, include major design changes or options early in the design process so the timeline and budget for the project is not severely impacted.

One of the most important duties of the church building committee will not only be to select and approve the architectural firm for the project, but to select the general contractor as well. Including members on the building committee that have prior experience in church construction is very helpful when it comes to this process. In the next chapter, I will discuss the general contractor selection process.

5

Selecting Your General Contractor

With the project manager and building committee in place, the budget estimated, the architect identified, and the church informed and approving the project, it is time to select a general contractor to construct the church building. The general contractor (GC) will bid the project, submit an estimate for the project, and subcontract with the various trades to complete the project (electrical, plumbing, HVAC, etc.). There are a variety of ways to add potential GCs to your list of candidates. One approach that has worked well for me in the past is to ask the architect to recommend several potential GCs. These would be GCs the architect has worked with previously and feels are qualified to complete the church's project. I would strongly recommend the church bid the construction contract with several GCs. This instills competition between the GCs for the project and motivates them to provide the best price they can deliver for the construction.

    I would recommend three to five GCs be on the final list to ask for bids. You may, for example, start out with six potential GCs and narrow the list down to three. But three to five potential GCs should provide enough bid competition to provide a good price for the church project. The PM will be a major part of contacting potential GCs and determining their interest in the construction. The PM should contact the GC and give them a general idea of the size, scope, and timeline of the project as well as some preliminary estimated cost for construction (as previously discussed, the architect can be helpful in determining this estimated construction cost).

It is very important the church thoroughly research the potential GCs and their capabilities. One thing the church needs to determine: does the GC have any experience in church construction? Just like the architect, this expertise can be very helpful if they are familiar with specific church requirements for a building. Also, ask for examples of their work, visit buildings the GC has constructed (especially churches), and interview people that have used that GC in their projects. Other PMs often came to me asking about the capabilities of GCs in my past projects and I often spoke to other PMs about potential GCs. So, do the legwork to vet potential GCs to assure they have the capabilities to do a good job on the church project.

Be prepared that some GCs may not have any interest in the church project since their plate may be full with other business, or the timeline of the church construction does not fit into their business schedule. This is why having three to five potential GCs on your list is helpful. Some of them will not be available for your project. Again, the information I typically provided to any contractor was the basic preliminary design provided by the architect, the estimated cost to build, and the timeline to be in the new building. The timeline for construction is often the driving factor in a GCs interest in the project. Given the age of technology, all of project information can be sent by email attachment and really helps speed up the communication process. Once you have determined which GCs are interested in the project, brief the building committee and church staff on the potential candidates. Allow the building committee and staff to make any final cuts to the list of potential GCs before requesting formal bids.

Let me interject something at this point, which is vital information to provide to the GC prior to bidding the construction project. If the church has purchased a building for renovation, it is essential (and in most areas is a requirement) to perform a lead and asbestos inspection of the building as well as termite inspection (especially if you live in an area where termites thrive). The GC will need to have this information in hand showing these inspections have been performed and the issues resolved before the GC can obtain a building permit. These inspections could require a considerable amount of lead time to accomplish and for the corrective action to take place. It is my experience the church will need to contract with one company, which only performs lead and asbestos inspections, and then contract with a separate company that actually performs the lead and asbestos abatement. The time required to bid separate companies for this task and then the actual timeline to get this work done can easily be a month or more. Termite inspections and treatment are a bit more straightforward, but should be done well prior to starting the bid process. So, do not delay having both inspections performed long before you start the process of bidding construction work for a new church project.

Once the building committee and church staff make their final cut to the GC list, the PM will need to draft a formal letter (on church letterhead) requesting bids for the project. I suggest the bid letter be sent to each individual contractor and not a mass mailing. This instills a feeling of personal contact and each letter should be signed by the PM. The contents of this letter and its attachments are very important in giving the bidding contractors all the information they need to submit an accurate bid. The important items, which should be included in the bid request letter, are:

Location and description of the new construction: State the location of the building, formal address, and the approximate size of the structure being built. Denote if this is new construction or renovation of an existing building. If it is a renovation, describe the exterior finish of the building, interior finishes, previous function of the building, and intended purpose of the new building. Note any important details such as location of new water lines if they are to be installed and if there are any water management or business association requirements that apply. Clearly state the desired "in building" date and the architectural firm for the project.

Proposal requirements: Inform the bidding contractor the building will be built to the specification of the architects drawing package. The bid letter will include an attachment on how to access the architect's drop box site so the contractor can review the current drawings and specifications. If the contractor takes any exception to the drawings or specifications they must be clearly stated in their bid proposal.

Bids: State the point of contact, date and time the bids should be returned, and the church address for submitting those bids (for example: April 28, 2017, 4 PM, 204 Jones Street, Big Town FL, at the church office). Inform the contractor in the letter the date of the contract award (for example: May 20, 2017) and that this will occur after a final approval of the church congregation. The contractor's written response, in five copies, should include the completed bid form.

Contractor Personnel: The bid letter should require the contractor to submit a list of expected subcontractors and name the contractor project manager and superintendent. For both of these individuals, the contractor should list their experience in the last five years with references.

Special Considerations: The bid letter will also include an attachment, which addresses items the contractor must agree to for the construction project. These may include but are not limited to: owner-provided items, lay down areas, access to the construction site and traffic restrictions, contractor-provided items/tasks, demolition, permitting, long-lead items, owner-installed items, contractor completion date confidence, builder's insurance, financial tracking, contractor schedule, liquidated damages, and designating Sunday as a non-work day.

Contract award: Inform the contractor that once bids are received, a lump sum contract will be awarded. The contract will be awarded on a "best fit" criteria:

1. A competitive price.
2. A highly qualified group of subcontractors based on references from recent jobs, which shows they can perform quality work on schedule.
3. A superintendent, not a foreman, with demonstrated experience and performance who can accomplish the job on schedule.

I strongly suggest a note be added after item three, which states, "Submitting the lowest price but failing to meet items two and/or three above will not result in contract award." The reason for this is obvious, the lowest bid may include subpar subcontractors to perform the work and therefore would negate the credibility of the lowest bid. Or, the superintendent may not be qualified in the church's view to oversee the project on-site. Include in the bid letter that the church reserves the right to conduct discussions (or negotiations) with any or all of the bidders.

Let me pause here to further expand on a few of the items contained in the special considerations attachment to the bid letter. The special considerations attachment allows the church to inform the bidding contractors of unique needs, processes, or constraints of the project and work site. First, let's look at "long-lead-time items." This refers to construction supplies such as steel beams and columns, custom glass for windows, etc., which require an extended time to be manufactured before being delivered for installation. The church states up front in the special considerations what items require a long lead time (the architect can advise on this), and the contractor is responsible for making sure these items are ordered well enough in advance to meet the construction timeline. If these items are not ordered in a timely manner, this will most likely result in a significant construction timeline delay due to the long lead times for delivery.

Next, let me discuss the "liquidated damages" provision of the special considerations. This is a provision where the contractor pays the church for each work day they exceed the completion deadline date for the project. In my past experience, this has been typically five hundred dollars per day. The reason for this is to allow the church to recoup lost costs incurred from missing the deadline date due to contractor management of the project. A church will no doubt plan a grand opening for the building, advertise on TV, radio, and billboards and have other significant costs in preparation for the grand opening. When the timeline slips, due to the contractor, then the church would incur advertisement lost costs and these would need to be recovered. In another example, the church will be taking delivery of all the furniture for the new building and if they cannot place the items in the building when required, then they will need to pay for storage. This is another lost cost to the church. Just like any other business, a church risks losing potential "customers" and incurring costs if they cannot open on time. Liquidated damages can only be enforced realistically if the delay is solely caused by the contractor's management of the project. An example of this would be a delay of construction materials, such as steel beams, which are under the complete control of the contractor. Delays caused by "hidden flaws" discovered during a demolition (such as termite or water damage) cannot be charged to the contractor as liquidated damages since the contractor is not directly responsible for unforeseen hidden flaws. Another example for not implementing liquidated damages would be damage and delay caused by severe weather (tornado, hurricane, etc.) Also, it is paramount the "work week" be defined for the liquidated damages period and stated clearly in the special instructions and in the contract. Typically this would be Monday through Friday, 8:00 a.m. to 4:00 p.m., and would include Saturday if liquid damages are implemented.

"Builder's insurance" is a required coverage for any new construction. It protects the owner from loss if the partially complete construction is destroyed by fire, weather, or natural disaster. The church undoubtedly has insurance on their existing building but this coverage does not extend to construction insurance. The church will be required to obtain builder's insurance coverage either through the general contractor or the church will need to purchase that insurance on their own for the project. The contractor can include builder's insurance in the construction contract with the church but will charge a 5-7 percent fee for that service. I recommend the church contact their existing insurance provider and obtain builder's insurance on their own. It will most likely be much cheaper. The church will be required to provide documentation to the contractor that they have builder's insurance before a building permit can be issued.

With all these details covered in the bid letter, it is now time to send out the bid letters to the potential general contractors and wait with anticipation for the day the bids are submitted to the church. Generally, a time period of two to three weeks, from the date of the bid letter to the bid opening date, is long enough for the contractor to do all the legwork needed to formulate the bid. Keep in mind the contractor will be studying the design, lining up subcontractors and obtaining bids from them, and possibly visiting the church construction site. During the bidding process, the bidding contractors may want to inspect the construction site to get a better feel for the lay of the land, the existing building, or the renovation involved. The PM should make the construction site available to all contractors who want to inspect the site prior to bidding. Expect the bidding contractors may need to return several times to inspect specific details on the work site to refine their bids. It is also a good idea to send the bid letters to the bidding contractor both by mail and by e-mail. In one of my past projects, I only sent the bid letters by mail and found out one of the contractors did not receive a letter. Fortunately when I sent them by mail, I always followed up with a phone call a day or two later to ensure the contractor had received the bid letter. It was after this occurrence that I began sending the bid letters by both mail and email.

Completing the bid letter, getting it sent by mail and e-mail to the competing contractors, sets the stage for the next event, which is the "bid day." This is the day when contractors submit their bids for review by the church. Frankly, this is one of the more exciting times for me and I can describe it as a combination of Christmas morning and the Fourth of July! The anticipation is infectious among the church staff and building committee as people try to predict the winning contractor for the project. Of course no one actually knows the winning bid until they are opened and reviewed by the building committee.

There are several ways to review the bids at submission, but the way I found that is the most ethical, above board, honest, and an approach that leaves no doubt about church integrity is to open the bids in front of all the competing contractors. Typically, I would set a time and place for the contractors to deliver their bids, a work day at 4:00 p.m., and in a designated room of the church. The people in attendance to receive the bids would be the building committee and of course the contractors submitting the bids.

In every bid process, it was always interesting to note that right up to 4:00 p.m., I could observe the contractors sitting in their cars, on their cell phones, finalizing their bids to the last minute. From their point of view, they wanted to be as accurate as possible in their bids. Since 4:00 p.m. would be the cut off time to receive bids, all contractors would be in the room at that time to submit their bids. With the building committee in place and the contractors in attendance, I would then open the bids and post all the bid numbers on the white board for all in attendance too see. This has one very valuable consequence in making the bid submittal open and honest and speaks of the church's integrity in the process. Also, it will give the contractors some immediate feedback on the ranking of their bids. I generally close the meeting by thanking the contractors for their bid packages and ask if there are any general questions for the church. I tell them, after a review of all the bids, the church will notify the contractors of the winning bid.

This is the point where the presence and participation of the building committee comes into focus for selecting the winning bid. The building committee will review the packages and evaluate the bids. As stated earlier in this chapter, the bid request letter states the "best fit" bid will be the one selected based on specific criteria. Therefore, having the lowest bid but having a poor subcontractor list or an unqualified contractor project manager or superintendent could negate the lowest bid. These are all things the building committee must review and resolve in the bid review process. Many times in the bid review process, the winning bid was clearly apparent within an hour of review of the submitted bids. However, the church should take the time it needs to appropriately review the bids, follow-up with questions to the contractors if needed, and be prepared to negotiate with the contractors on specific details. Recall the bid letter did state the church reserved the right to negotiate with any and all contractors in the bid process.

Once the winning bid is selected, and the church congregation has given their vote of approval, it will be the church project manager's task to notify the winners and the non-winners of the bid. I state it exactly in those terms since you don't want to refer to any contractor as a "loser." The contractors provided a full-faith effort on their bid and on their company's time. So, the church project manager should be diplomatic in notifying the winner and non-winners. Typically, I would make a personal phone call to the winning contractor, as well as the non-winning contractors, and then follow up the notifications with a letter on church letterhead. Keep in mind the church might have another construction project in the future. And, the church wants to keep a good rapport with all contractors who submitted bids for the church's project. These business contacts can be very valuable for future projects.

Just as with the architectural contract, the project manager, building committee, and church staff need to review and understand the conditions of the construction contract. Items included in the contract will include the names of the church and the primary contractor, the location of the work site, type construction to be performed (new construction, renovation, etc.), and the architect of record. The construction contract will also denote the date of commencement for the work and the number of days to substantial completion of the project. If the church elects to include liquidated damages in the contract, then this verbiage should be included as well. The contract will clearly state the contract sum for the project with the base bid plus any alternative options and values (such as the option to remove all drywall, entry storefront replacement, etc.). The contract will also include procedures for such items as progress payments and dispute resolution. Typically, the architectural firm is responsible for drafting the contract between the owner and contractor using the American Institute of Architects (AIA) Standard Form of Agreement.

One final note in this chapter has to do with church integrity. As Christians representing the Body of Christ, we much exude fair play, honesty, and ethical behavior above all else. Nothing can kill a church's reputation quicker than unethical business dealings or behavior. Always be above board, be truthful, and be fair in dealing with the community. A church with an ethical business reputation will never lack for contractors clambering to do business with that type of church.

6

Church-Managed Subcontractors

Competing the construction project, selecting the winning bid, and having a construction contract in place is a major milestone in the process. The general contractor can now oversee the work of all the subcontractors necessary to complete the work. However, the church may elect to contract directly with specific subcontractors for detailed or highly technical work in the new building. In my past projects areas the church subcontracted directly, and which the church project manager oversaw, it included interior wall theming for the children's areas, audio/visual equipment and installation, signage, theatrical lighting, and landscaping.

The reasons for managing these subcontracts outside the general contract were varied. However, the reasons were usually related to specific technical ability of the subcontractor, or the subcontractor was a member of the church and would provide the work at a much reduced cost on labor, parts, or product. This approach worked well in most cases and having subcontractors that were church members made them usually very easy to work with during the construction.

But, there can be some downsides to contracting directly with subcontractors for the construction project. The general rule is the more you can leave on the plate for the general contractor to manage the fewer management headaches for the church or project manager.

It will be the project manager's additional duty to manage church subcontractors. The project manager's duties are already rather significant, and adding too many subcontractors for him to manage will take time away from his time to oversee the entire project. I would recommend three or four church-managed subcontracts, which should be enough for any project.

Also, the general contractor is responsible for the timeline and finishing the project on time. Therefore, he has to make sure all of his subcontractors are completing their work on time and on schedule. Once the church starts managing specific subcontractors, then the church, and especially the project manager, is responsible for seeing the church subcontractors are expeditiously completing the work and will not hold up the general contractor's timeline. This could have a very significant impact on things such as implementing liquidated damages. If the church managed-subcontractors are responsible for slow work, and causing the timeline to slip past the finish date, then the church cannot implement liquidated damages against the general contractor for missing the deadline. Again, this emphasizes why it is important to leave as much subcontractor work under the general contractor's control as possible.

Let me address one other issue about selecting subcontractors for the construction project. It is a good rule of thumb that if the church needs a specific contractor service for the project (exterminator, lead/asbestos inspection, etc.), it is best to get two or three bids for that service. It is the goal of the church to get the best price for the money. However, collecting bids does take time and would require the project manager to again divide his time between construction oversight and soliciting bids. If the church already has a company under contract for a needed service (such as an exterminator), then the church should first contact that company for a quote to perform the work. If the project manager or building committee feels the quote is unreasonable, then implement the bid process for an exterminator. The point here is to save time by not soliciting bids when the best price might already be established with a company providing a service to the church. Soliciting bids for services should be used when there is clearly no known price for the required service.

Let me make one final comment about charitable contributions of project building materials (fill dirt, sod, landscaping, etc.) made by members of the church. These are all wonderful gifts and can be very beneficial to the church in saving money for materials that might otherwise be acquired at cost through the general contractor. But there is one very important consideration about these gifts that the church staff must keep in mind. If these donations of materials cannot be delivered to the work site when they are needed, they really are not helpful to the project. Just like any other subcontractor, these "subcontracted" gifts must arrive in time to be installed to meet the milestones and deadline of the project. This is even more important if the donated materials are a very significant part of the construction. It is my opinion, since these are charitable gifts to the church, the senior church staff should coordinate these gifts directly and oversee the delivery of these material donations to assure they meet project timelines.

7

Starting the Construction

Up to this point, you may have the impression the church project manager (PM) is a very busy person and indispensable to the church in managing the construction project. And you would be very correct in that assumption! However, with the actual start of construction at the work site, the PM is now going to have a considerable increase in his work load and it will continue to ramp up until the project is complete. The first sign of this is the absolute need for the PM to be on site every day to oversee the construction. Prior to this time, most issues could be worked from home at a desk. But now, being in the field to be the "eyes and ears" of the church and being a problem solver is a major aspect of the PM's work day.

Even from the very first day of construction having a PM on-site, who is authorized and capable to answer questions or provide guidance as "the owner," is paramount to the overall success of the project. My point of view was I spoke for the owner and I represented the church in making sure the project was meeting architectural design specifications. And, I was there to observe consistent progress was being made to meet the project timeline and milestones. An involved and dedicated PM will be the first to know if construction is not going to plan or if the project is falling behind schedule. This involves periodic updates to the building committee and church staff keeping them informed of the construction process. For me, that usually meant a monthly update to a church administrative board and weekly, and sometimes daily updates, to the church building committee. Generally, the questions that were most often asked were: "Are we on time?" and "Are we on budget?"

Let me also say, with the start of actual on-site construction, people need to be able to reach the PM for coordination or questions. At the very least, a PM needs a cell phone to coordinate all the construction details that take place during construction. And if this is a renovation or new construction, about the only way to communicate from the work site is by cell phone. A typical work day for the PM is filled with phone conversations with the architect, general contractor project manager, various church-managed subcontractors, and church leadership. As a point of reference, I was on site each day at 7:00 a.m. and typically departed around 3:00-4:00 p.m. But at times I was there earlier or later depending on the circumstances. I would often receive construction-related calls driving to the work site in the mornings, returning home from the work site in the evenings, and calls throughout the day.

The first week of the actual construction is really the "honeymoon" period for the construction phase. Everyone will be upbeat and ready to start the project, everything is under control, and there is very little to worry about on the work site at that point. But very soon, the actual hard work on the site will begin and everyone will start earning their pay to see that construction specifications, timeline, and budget are being met. I started each day talking with the contractor's superintendent to see what was on the construction agenda for that day. It is so very important to have a good rapport with the superintendent since he is the contractor's agent for directing the construction on-site. I was fortunate to have good superintendents on most of my past projects and this can make the oversight of the project a real pleasure.

However, sometimes, despite the interviews, references, and recommendations, a project can end up with the wrong superintendent. It won't take long to see the contractor has the wrong man to lead the job. Personality conflicts, lack of attention to detail, poor decisions, and bad attitude are all death nails for the project if the superintendent exhibits these traits during the construction. It will get to the point the project will start languishing in any kind of substantial progress and the morale of the site will be in turmoil. A bad superintendent is an infectious virus, which spreads through all the subcontractors as they start losing faith in his decision-making capabilities. When the church project manager can no longer work with the contractor's superintendent because of these issues, a meeting with the contractor's project manager and/or owner is warranted and needed. Most likely the best result is to replace the poorly performing superintendent and rebuild the work site and its morale. I have found this was the solution on past projects and it allowed the construction to move ahead in a positive manner.

One of the most important meetings at the construction site are the periodic visits by the architect to check on the progress of the construction. For my projects, we would have a contractor-architect-owner meeting every two weeks to inspect the site, compare status of the work to the contractor's schedule, and discuss and determine solutions for any on-site construction issues. The architect typically has a keen eye and can readily spot problems that may not be seen by the contractor or owner. The architect's presence on-site is very helpful in determining solutions for problems or helping to head off problems before they occur.

One example of this occurred during placement of two new HVAC units adjacent to a newly renovated building. These were large units, which supplied the heating and cooling to the sanctuary. Each of them weighed several thousand pounds and were designed to sit on concrete pads. However, the part of the lot behind the building, where the units were to be placed, was narrow and had an obvious drainage problem. And if these HVAC units were placed on the concrete platforms as designed, the rainwater would be dammed up behind the building and quite possibly flow into the building. I specifically asked the architect to visit the work site to find a solution to the problem. Ultimately, the architect's solution, made with valuable inputs from a member of the building committee, was to elevate the HVAC units on concrete rails thereby allowing the rainwater to drain underneath the units to the curb. It was an ideal solution!

It is important to have the regular meetings with the architect, and I would recommend nothing less than once every two weeks. Also, it is very appropriate to invite the lead subcontractors for a specialty (electrical, HVAC, plumbing, etc.) to these meetings to answer specific questions, provide updates, or resolve problems. However, if the size of your project demands more attention, weekly meetings with the contactor and architect are in order. And, if there is a significant problem the church project manager thinks requires expert attention, never hesitate to call the architect to the site to visually observe the problem and determine the fix. Allowing a problem to fester will only lead to lost time and ultimately a greater cost to the church.

Let me mention a rather novel issue that is important to everyone on the work site and that is portable toilets or the commonly seen "porta-potty." The general contractor is responsible for supplying an adequate number of portable toilets for the construction crew. Typically, one portable toilet is supplied for every ten workers on-site. Clearly, the toilets are needed if this is new construction or the complete renovation of an older building. The portable toilets are supplied for construction use and workers are not to use church facilities (this is a requirement made by the contractor). Given that a happy workforce is a productive workforce, I kept an eye on that ten-persons-per-toilet requirement to make sure we had adequate toilet facilities on-site. I also watched to make sure the toilet company routinely came by to service the toilets. If the church project manager notices there are not enough toilets on-site, or they are not being serviced in a timely manner, ask the superintendent to remedy the matter. Morale among the workers on the construction site is very important and the proper maintenance and number of toilets can be important to that morale.

BUILDING A CHURCH

At most at any construction site, dumpsters are needed to collect the construction waste, which occurs. Or, in the case of a renovation and demolition of the interior of the building, these dumpsters are vital in clearing the demolition waste off the site. The dumpsters often contain hazards that should preclude "dumpster diving" by people looking for salvageable materials. Typically, the dumpsters are well behind a construction fence and the fence is posted as a construction zone and no trespassing zone. It is the general contractor's responsibility to dissuade people from dumpster diving and the church should support this for the possible hazards that are involved. But occasionally, people will slip by to use the dumpsters not only to glean salvage but to dump their trash as well.

One morning, I arrived at the work site early and noticed a vacuum sweeper on top of the waste in a dumpster. This dumpster was behind the orange construction fence with the no trespassing sign clearly in view. As I investigated further, I was able to determine apparently during the night someone had cleaned out their apartment and dumped much of their old furniture and household items in the dumpster. Now here is the problem; construction waste is a very specific type waste that is allocated to the landfills. And, the contractor is charged as much as additional three hundred dollars per load for a dumpster that contains material that is not considered construction waste (concrete, metal, drywall, etc.) This extra fee is charged because at the landfill site, the material must be resorted and distributed to the correct area of the landfill. I sorted through the apartment material in the dumpster and ran across a shipping box that had the individuals name, address, phone number, and email address! So, at 7:00 a.m. that morning, I was happy to call the individual and inform him he needed to immediately remove his trash from the dumpster since he had illegally dumped. The individual was there within an hour and removed his trash. I informed him that by law construction, dumpsters are not "public" dumpsters and he was enlightened.

On another church project, the church was expanding the sanctuary, adding a wing to the children's building, and adding a new parking lot. Since the church property was immediately adjacent to wetlands, a large retention pond needed to be constructed to prevent water runoff from the new parking lot draining directly into the wetlands. To accomplish this task, the job required four thousand square yards of fill dirt to build the retention pond plus provide a viable base for the new wing of the building. To give the reader some idea of the amount of dirt that is required, the largest dump trucks you might see on the road are usually twenty-yard trucks. This means the job required two hundred loads of dirt from a truck this size to accomplish the task! The dirt was spread over two acres of land and the retention pond had to be built on sloping land to be effective. The pond was initially constructed in place and was holding water. But before the sides of the pond could be dressed in sod, the area experienced record rains those few weeks and the pond was at times brim full. One morning after a heavy night of rain, I arrived at the work site to see the side of the pond had been breached and the water unfortunately had drained into the wetlands. Bright and early that same morning, the water management inspectors were on site asking how we intended to fix the problem. If we did not meet the requirements for protecting the wetlands, the contractor would face a ten thousand-dollar-fine. We managed to come up with a plan and avoid the fine, but it was a stressful time until the pond was repaired and the wetlands were properly protected with silt fences and hay bales.

People arriving at a work site to view the construction can often be a hazard. Church members have been asked to pray for, and financially support, the new construction project and most of them truly have a vested interest in what was happening as the church expanded. They were anxious to see the progress and wanted to be able to view the progress first hand. This is clearly understandable, but on a construction work site, church members cannot just roam in and out at will. Often, the work site will be designated a "hard hat" area for very good reason especially if there is considerable overhead work involving wood and steel. It can be a very dangerous place. Also, OSHA requirements mandate the attire for the work site is hard hats, long pants, and closed-toe shoes if not steel-toe boots. It is important to remember that while this is a church project, financed and owned by the church, during construction the general contractor "owns" the site for construction. He is responsible for safety and is liable for any injuries during construction. For these reasons, it is best not to have church people roaming into the work site during construction. However, I did make provisions for special circumstances. I would have a few extra hard hats available when senior church staff or members of the building committee would need to view the work site. And I would make them aware of the proper attire to enter the work site. Sometimes, at the end of the work day when all workers were off site, I might arrange to take a few people in the building to view the progress, but always advising them of the proper clothing and especially proper shoes. I strongly advise it is not a good idea to allow church people in the work site during the full shift of the work day.

I provided the previous examples, based on past experiences at the construction work site, to give the reader an idea of the many issues and concerns the church project manager deals with on a daily basis. There is ongoing problem solving throughout the life of the project and this is just part of the daily construction routine. As I mentioned previously, each construction project takes on its own personality. However, there are things that will happen during the construction phase that will make you smile while others will cause despair. But, starting your day with prayer, seeking God's guidance, and asking for strength and wisdom will help you face each day to overcome and persevere to the end of your project.

8

The Dreaded Change Order

A change order is a process that identifies something, which needs to be added or changed in the design of the building during construction to make the building safer, function more effectively, or to meet building codes. Most commonly, the church will discover they have left something out of the original design, which is needed in the building to make the building more functional (such as adding water fountains in the children's area of the new building). The important point about understanding the change order process is any addition to the design will cost the church more money, and in many cases, more time. Change orders during construction cannot be eliminated, but they can be cut down in their number by proper preplanning of the building in the design phase.

 Some change orders are simply unavoidable. In my most recent project, the church was renovating a fourteen thousand-square foot, two story building. And even though we had a thorough termite inspection, we found even more significant termite damage after all the drywall was removed from the interior of the building. And, given that the building previously had been a health club with Jacuzzis and saunas, there was considerable water damage in the walls of the building adjacent to those areas. Needless to say, these hidden flaws required change orders with a substantial amount of repair and cost.

The change order will be addressed by the general contractor and he will provide the church with an estimate for the repair. I always informed the building committee and staff of the change order and the cost to repair. In most cases, this is just a straightforward process since the repair is required to move forward with the project.

I do want to emphasize again, many of the potential change orders can be avoided, if the church takes a reasonable amount of time to develop the design and includes church experts in reviewing the preliminary design plans. If the church is building a new children's wing, then by all means include the children's minister and staff in the planning. Their experience will be vital in designing the most functional children's areas. And this will help eliminate the need for a change order to add an item during construction not included in the original design.

The change order is also one of the primary reasons the church needs to maintain a contingency fund as part of the church construction budget. You just don't know what might happen during construction that would require a change order and the funds to fix a problem in the design or a hidden flaw. As I mentioned in the project budgeting section of the book, I feel a contingency fund of 10 percent of the construction budget is realistic to deal with unforeseen costs. However, there will be some in the church staff, and especially in the financial staff, that may want to reduce the 10 percent number. Just keep in mind, it is more beneficial to have budgeted contingency money on hand that the church *does not need* as opposed to needing money the church *does not have*.

9

Time, Quality, Money

I would like to turn now to a brief discussion of a rather simple relationship in the construction process, which is all too often misunderstood. It is the relationship of time, quality, and money in regards to the project and how they interact with each other. Basically, the project has a set amount of time from beginning to completion, a determined amount of money to complete the project, and a desired quality product to meet the needs and function of the church. Each one of these facets, if changed, will have a definite effect on the other two.

Suppose the church contracts for a six-month timeline to complete the renovation of a fourteen thousand-square-foot building. This is a rather aggressive timeline by any measure and does not allow for any major obstacles to occur during the construction. And also suppose during the construction, the church discovers considerable termite and water damage (this should sound familiar) and it will require a change order to fix the problems. The timeline will now slip from 15 November to 15 December, since it will require extra time for the contractor to fix these hidden flaws. Not only is the timeline affected by a slip, but the hidden flaws will result in additional money to correct the problem. However, the one facet that may have not been affected negatively is the quality. The quality of the project is assured and possibly increased by repairing the damage. So in this example, time is lengthened, money needs are increased, but quality is maintained or enhanced by the added change order repair.

Now, imagine (and I'm giving a fictitious example in this case) the church has a tight six-month schedule for the same fourteen thousand-square foot building and wants to be in the building one month earlier for some particular reason. The only way to do this would be to pay the contractor for twenty-four-hour operations to complete the project and be in the building thirty days sooner. While time might be reduced, and seen as a benefit by the church, I assure you that the church would pay much more in cost to have the project completed early. Quality could remain the same, but rushing the project to completion would most likely degrade the quality of the final product. So in this example, being in the building earlier is seen as a time benefit while costing the church more money and possibly degrading the quality of the product.

The point I want the reader to take away from this brief discussion is if the church makes arbitrary decisions about construction, without considering the interrelationship of time, quality, and money, at least one of the three facets will be affected negatively. And, they will probably be affected to the detriment of the project. So in all cases, the church leadership, building committee, and project manager should keep in mind this interrelationship to avoid unnecessary and negative impacts on time, quality, and money.

10

Racing to Completion and the Certificate of Occupancy

Typically about mid-way through the construction, to the completion of the project, the pace of the construction rises to a fever pitch. These are the days the project manager is finding his daily routine is full of construction coordination, decision making, and expediting the project to completion. This is also the time the church project manager can easily find himself putting in twelve-hour days due to the demands of the construction. It can be a very exciting time to see the project nearing completion, but it can also be a very stressful time. This is when I found prayer to be an essential part of my daily routine to help me persevere to the end.

One of the inevitable issues, which always occurred on my past projects, was coordinating furniture deliveries at just the right time to be placed in the new building. Lead times for furniture can vary greatly based on the type of furniture and the providing company. In my experience, the church could find the best deals for its money if it ordered building furniture on its own and took this task out of the hands of the general contractor (and I do highly recommend this). But, ordering furniture can also be a very time intensive process if you use volunteers in the church. To give the reader some idea of the amount of furniture needed in a renovated fourteen thousand-square-foot building, this project required 320 cushioned sanctuary chairs, 100 metal chairs for two worship area rooms, tables and chairs for four classrooms (toddler through fifth grade), infant furniture for babies and crawlers, area rugs, movable storage cabinets, washer/dryer, and office furniture for three offices, and this is just a partial list!

I have managed furniture orders in two ways in past projects, one way by using dedicated volunteers and the other was to subcontract a furniture resource company to manage ordering furniture. Both approaches were successful, but I found the larger the building size and the more furniture needed, the furniture resource company was the best approach. In dealing with a furniture resource company, I had to coordinate with only one person in making sure the furniture was being ordered and would arrive at the appropriate time. In case of numerous volunteers, I had to coordinate with a group of people and at times it was hard to determine exactly who was responsible for ordering what items and who was tracking the finances. Dealing with the furniture resource company was especially advantageous if the timeline slipped and the furniture needed to be delayed, or if the furniture delivery date needed to be moved up. For a smaller project, the volunteer approach can work well, but for a larger project such as construction of a new church or renovated building being turned into a church, I strongly recommend contracting with a furniture resource company to order furniture. The church will need to subcontract with the furniture resource company and pay a fee for their services.

Even with the best coordination, melding furniture delivery times into the construction timeline will be difficult at best. The target date for being in the building is called the "Certificate of Occupancy" date or "CO" date. It is the date the project is substantially complete and the church is authorized to occupy the building and conduct operations. But, before this can happen, there are a myriad of final inspections by the city or county, which include life safety by the fire marshal, electrical, plumbing, HVAC, etc., all of which must be passed before the city or county can sign off on the CO. So, if the planned target date to obtain the CO is 15 November, then all furniture deliveries must be slated to arrive on 16 November or later. It should be fairly obvious that any kind of delays in the schedule can greatly affect furniture deliveries. Very simply, if you cannot determine the CO date, it is hard to schedule furniture deliveries on an unknown date.

One possible solution, one that worked for me on previous projects, was to work with the general contractor to store some furniture in the building on a non-interference basis. This will require negotiation with the contractor and, quite frankly, the church is very lucky of the general contractor agrees to this arrangement. As I mentioned in previous chapters, the general contractor "owns" the site for construction until the issuance of the CO, which formally turns the building over to the church for operations. Therefore, if the furniture is stored in the building prior to the CO, the general contractor could be held responsible for damage or theft. Not many contractors would be willing to take that risk. The only other viable solution would be for the church to store furniture until it can be moved into the new building. But of course, this would be an extra cost to the church.

The dilemma for the church, and even the furniture resource company, is the furniture lead times and variations in delivery dates by supplying companies. Some companies want to deliver within a week of ordering, others will want to deliver within thirty days or less. This can be a nightmare of logistics for the church trying to coordinate a moving CO date with inflexible furniture delivery dates. In some of my projects, I relied on a combination of solutions, which included storing some furniture in the new building (with the general contractors consent) and storing furniture near the site for move in by volunteers after the CO date.

Many of the church members will not truly understand the nature of the CO and while the building may look like it's ready for occupancy, it actually is not. Until all the final inspections are performed by city/county inspectors, life safety has been performed by the fire marshal, and the church actually has a CO in hand, the building cannot be used by the church for any "gathering" purposes. So as much as church groups would like to be in the building to conduct training or get volunteers familiar with the layout of the building, they must wait until after the CO is issued. If the church tries to occupy the building prior to the issuance of the CO, they can face penalties from the city/county agencies.

In the race to completion, the project manager will find that all the trades can be working on top of each other to complete the construction. It is typical to have the flooring, painters, cabinet installers, and other trades all working in a very small space. This is also the time when the project manager makes very important decisions for the church on trim and fit. I suppose I could make as many as twenty decisions a day on these type issues. Such decisions might include where a floor trim line should end, where a paint line should start between two paint colors, or if a cabinet needs to be shifted for an appropriate fit. At this point, I found I also functioned as a decision maker, expediter, coordinator, referee, and traffic cop! I functioned many times as a traffic cop for items delivered to the work site, helping eighteen-wheel semitrucks back into the work site from a busy road, blocking traffic until the semitruck was in place.

Once the CO is issued, the church can fully start moving into the building and conducting all of the operations of the church. There still may be some minor construction taking place, but the church volunteers and staff can begin the operations they have been anxiously waiting to start. Issuance of the CO is a very major milestone in the life of the construction project. It is the final point that major construction ends and only minor touch up tasks are being performed. One example of this might be light fixtures being installed by the electrical subcontractor. At times, even the subcontractors experience delivery delays in specially designed products. They may need to return to install the correct design lighting fixtures in place of temporary fixtures. Another example might be the plumbing subcontractor returning to replace a toilet tank, with the flush handle on the correct side, for a handicapped restroom. These are all examples of the kinds of contractor work that can occur post-CO.

Ultimately, from the point of view of the church and the project manager, obtaining the CO means the project is very near completion. This will start much of the "close-out" process for the project manager as pay applications are made to the general contractor and invoices are paid to the church managed subcontractors. The project manager would be the one to authorize and direct payment to church managed subcontractors through financial accounts set up for that purpose by the church accountant. Needless to say, the project manager should always have a feel for the overall budget, if construction is staying within the planned budget, and if the accounts are not being overspent.

11

Post Construction Maintenance and the Warranty

Let's look now at the post construction issue of maintenance and warranty. With the issuance of the Certificate of Occupancy (CO), this begins the one-year building warranty provided by the general contractor. It is important to confirm with both the architect and general contractor that the CO date is the start date for the warranty. In some cases, the warranty start date could be the substantial completion date (which can occur a few weeks prior to the CO date), but in the view of the church, it should actually be the CO date since this is the date the church is legally authorized to be in the building. The church and project manager needs to iron out this detail with the architect and general contractor once the CO is issued.

It is also during this step of the process that the architect, contractor, and project manager will conduct the "punch list" of items that need to be repaired. This is essentially the final walk through of the building identifying those items that require repair by specific subcontractors (plumbing, electrical, cabinet, flooring, painters, etc.) For a large construction project, this can be a rather lengthy list that includes such things as scratches in wall paint, loose floor tiles, poor fit and trim on cabinets, and leaking faucets. The punch list is also a final process step for both the architect and contractor and they will coordinate a date for the punch list walk through with the project manager. The punch list is very helpful in identifying post construction problems that could be covered later under the building warranty.

The warranty date is good for one year on the new building and any failure in the building, due to construction, requires repair to full service by the general contractor. It is imperative the church quickly forwards discrepancies to the contractor for repair and it is just as imperative the general contractor responds in a timely manner. One very important aspect to this process, from the church's point of view, is to have a designed point-of-contact at the church who manages warranty issues. Typically, this would be the church building/facilities manager designated for the building. All warranty discrepancies would be filtered through this individual to be passed on to the general contractor. I found both a phone call to the general contractor and a follow-up e-mail was best to assure the message was received. Also, when reporting the discrepancy, include pictures of the problem if necessary, and be as concise as possible in describing the problem so the contractor can send the appropriate technician to perform the repair.

It could be the project manager will end up filling the role of facilities manager for the new church building post-CO. The project manager's knowledge of the building would be invaluable in determining the problems that need to be repaired under the warranty. However, if the church is a multicampus church, and especially if the project manager is located a great distance from the new construction, it would be best to have someone located close to the new building to act as the facilities manager. I'm certain a responsible project manager would be happy to advise on warranty maintenance issues after completing his duties as the project manager.

The warranty is a vital part of the construction process after the CO is issued. It is so very important the church stay on top of warranty maintenance issues to make sure the building is delivered and operating as designed. One important caution here, any damage caused by the church during this warranty period is not the responsibility of the general contractor. So, the facilities manager should initially determine the nature of the problem whether it is a warranty issue covered by the general contractor or a problem caused by church misuse (window broken by a baseball, holes gouged in the walls during move in, etc.)

12

Celebrate Your Success!

Now is the time for a gloriously rewarding point in the life of a construction project! It is the time you celebrate the completion and formal grand opening of the new building with the church and the community. I must say, I have enjoyed showing off the building to people after a project completion and, with humble pride, show them how all the efforts of many people have culminated into a good work! It is very rewarding to watch the faces of people that are seeing the building for the first time and marveling at the finishes and functionality of the final product. These reactions instill lifelong memories. It is also very rewarding to see how well received the final product is with the church congregation as well as members of the community.

There are many ways to celebrate the success, but the most important way is to have a grand opening ceremony for the building usually on a Sunday morning. All kinds of festivities can be planned to show off the building; perhaps a grand opening celebration during Sunday services followed by an open house that afternoon. People love to see the new building in actual operation as much as quietly viewing the building in an open house walk through. Having church staff members there to show the building and explain the operations of the new areas is very enlightening to people as they walk through the building.

One other very important way to advertise the new building is to have a separate day to invite city/county leaders, mayors, councilmen, business community leaders, and area clergy leaders to view the new facility. Often, many of these people were directly involved in city or county planning and coordination for the project and they too would be very happy to view the final product. This would be more of a formal affair and the church may want to cater refreshments for the dignitaries that attend the formal viewing. There is another very important reason for having these type viewings and open houses; it may very well bring someone into the church that may otherwise have never attended. And, after seeing the finished product, they may very well want to return to attend the new church or facility. Many churches have found that people are much more likely to attend a new church building.

This is also a time of giving thanks to God for strength and perseverance in completing a church construction project. I assure you, a devoted project manager will learn his strengths and weaknesses in a large construction project and will come out much more humble on the other side. And after committing to a project for a year or longer, it may also be necessary to take time to get your personal, spiritual, and worship life back in balance, and, by all means, take time to do so! And, you may also find in all of your projects, the very last thing you ever expected, would be to pass on a legacy to other people by authoring a "how to" book for navigating the church construction process! May God bless you in the success of your construction project, and I hope you too will be spiritually rewarded for a job "well done!"

About the Author

Terry Harpool is a long time resident of northwest Florida and a retired military officer (Lt. Colonel, USAF). He served as a church project manager for several construction projects in Okaloosa County, Florida including additions, renovations, and new construction. He is a member of the First Baptist Church in Crestview, Florida.

www.ingramcontent.com/pod-product-compliance
Lightning Source LLC
Chambersburg PA
CBHW021025180526
45163CB00005B/2120